THE CRAP FAMILY XMAS BIBLE

A Seasonal Sneer To All That's Crap About Christmas!

THE CRAP FAMILY XMAS BIBLE

A Seasonal Sneer To All That's Crap About Christmas!

By Ruth Graham   Cartoons by Gill Toft

www.knowthescorebooks.com

Know The Score Books Limited
118 Alcester Road
Studley
Warwickshire
B80 7NT
01527 454482
info@knowthescorebooks.com

A CIP catalogue record is available for this book from the British Library   ISBN: 978-1-905449-21-7

Jacket and book design by Lisa David
Cartoons by Gill Toft

Printed and bound in Great Britain by Martins The Printer

"I'm dreaming of a shite Christmas..."

CONTENTS

"The one thing women don't want to find in their stockings on Christmas morning is their husband." – Joan Rivers

The Supreme Court has ruled that they cannot have a nativity scene in Washington, D.C. This wasn't for any religious reasons. They couldn't find three wise men and a virgin.

~ Jay Leno

There has been only one Christmas - the rest are anniversaries.

~ W.J. Cameron

Roses are reddish
Violets are bluish
If it weren't for Christmas
We'd all be Jewish.

~ Benny Hill

You might as well do your Christmas hinting early.

~ Anonymous

Selfishness makes Christmas a burden, love makes it a delight.

~ Unknown

I once bought my kids a set of batteries for Christmas with a note on it saying: 'toys not included'.

~ Bernard Manning

There is a remarkable breakdown of taste and intelligence at Christmas time. Mature, responsible grown men wear neckties made of holly leaves and drink alcoholic beverages with raw egg yolks and cottage cheese in them.

~ P.J. O'Rourke

Never worry about the size of your Christmas tree.
In the eyes of children, they are all thirty feet tall.

~ Larry Wilde

Mail your packages early so the post office can lose
them in time for Christmas.

~ Johnny Carson

Oh dear. This high infant mortality rate's a real devil when it comes to staging quality children's theatre.

~ Lord Edmund Blackadder, on the dilemma of the nativity play, Blackadder's Christmas Carol

Next to a circus there ain't nothing that packs up and tears out faster than the Christmas spirit.

~ Kin Hubbard

Once again we find ourselves enmeshed in the Holiday Season, that very special time of year when we join with our loved ones in sharing centuries-old traditions such as trying to find a parking space at the mall. We traditionally do this in my family by driving around the parking lot until we see a shopper emerge from the mall, then we follow her, in very much the same spirit as the Three Wise Men, who 2000 years ago followed a star, week after week, until it led them to a parking space.

– Dave Barry

Christmas begins about the first of December with an office party – and ends when you finally realize what you spent, around April fifteenth of the next year.

– P.J. O'Rourke

Aren't we forgetting the true meaning of Christmas? You know, the birth of Santa.

– Bart Simpson

Oh look, yet another Christmas TV special! How touching to have the meaning of Christmas brought to us by cola, fast food, and beer... Who'd have ever guessed that product consumption, popular entertainment, and spirituality would mix so harmoniously?

~ Bill Watterson

I trust Christmas brings to you its traditional mix of generosity and violent stomach cramp.

~ Lord Edmund Blackadder,
(Blackadder's Christmas Carol)

No room in the inn? Well, that's 'cos it was Christmas innit!

~ Ali G

CHRISTMAS IS FOR KIDS

Just 14 more hours 'til bedtime...

True Christmas Letters

(with thanks to christmassantaclaus.com and several teachers who shall remain nameless)

Dear Santa
As my brother has been a very, very, very bad boy I would like you to send someone to torture him. Maybe a chunk of coal too. Bring my parents some neat stuff and the bill.

~ Holly, 9, Toledo, Ohio

Dear Santa
I am going to try to remember to wear my undies every day and not go commando to school.

~ Braedon, 8, Werribee, Australia

Dear Santa
Your reindeers get round very fast. Are they eco-friendly?

~ Sara, Bournemouth

Dear Santa
Nanny has been putting ideas in my ears, so this list is very long. An ipod would be good, and a new Playstation game too. Plus some cool trainers. Sorry if this sounds greedy. I won't ask for much next year. Thanks

~ Wayne, London

Dear Santa
My dog needs a girl dog because he is very lonely.

~ Katie, 6, Austin, Texas

Dear Santa
Do you know JESUS is the real reason of Christmas?
Not to be mean, but he is.

~ Rosanne, 11, Wrens, Georgia

Dear Santa
Could you get me some chocolate while you are over
Belgium?

~ Shane, London

Dear Santa
I want a DOG DOG DOG DOG DOG DOG DOG DOG
DOG DOG DOG DOG DOG DOG DOG DOG DOG DOG
DOG DOG DOG DOG DOG DOG DOG DOG DOG DOG
DOG DOG DOG DOG DOG DOG DOG DOG DOG DOG
DOG DOG.

~ Shaun, 10, Mississippi

Dear Santa
I could sure use some suggestions about what to get
my wife. Has she sent you any ideas?

~ Dale, 43

Dear Santa
What I'd really like is for my husband's ex-wife to be banished to the outer North Pole, with no telephone in sight. But I that know miracles are someone else's jurisdiction.

- Cierra, 42

SANTA'S CEASED TO BE

*"I stopped believing in Santa Claus when I was six.
Mother took me to see him in a department store and he
asked for my autograph."* – Shirley Temple

It was once said there are three stages:

You believe in Father Christmas,
You don't believe in Father Christmas,
You are Father Christmas.

To hurry the middle stage along and stop any tiresome children whining on about leaving out cookies and listening for reindeer on the roof, remind them of the following.

Santa has 31 hours of Christmas to work with, thanks to the different time zones and the rotation of the earth, assuming he travels east to west (which seems logical, otherwise he really would be pushing it). This works out to 822.6 visits per second.

This is to say that for each Christian household with good children, Santa has 1/1000th of a second to park, hop out of the sleigh, jump down the chimney, fill the stockings, distribute the remaining presents under the tree, eat whatever snacks have been left, get back up the chimney, get back into the sleigh and move on to the next house.

If each of these 91.8 million stops were evenly distributed around the earth (which they're not), we are now talking about .78 miles per household, a total trip of 75.5 million miles, not counting stops to do what most of us must do at least once every 31 hours, plus feeding etc.

This means that Santa's sleigh is moving at 650 miles per second, 3,000 times the speed of sound. For purposes of comparison, the fastest man-made vehicle invented on earth, the Ulysses space probe, trundles along at a sluggish 27.4 miles per second.

....Which surely all goes to prove that Santa's about as real as George Bush's English teacher. Get over it!

Real-life Disappointment Stories

My father was a doctor, and my mother his assistant. On Christmas Eve, I woke up and went downstairs, to find my mother filling sacks in the surgery for me and the others. I was so disappointed – I'd asked for a Reindeer, and just knew they couldn't get one in a sack, so realised then that Father Christmas was a lie.

– Lucy, London

The day I saw my mom eating the Santa cookies on the plate we'd left was one of the most horrific days of my life. I never let her forget it. I had at least three more good years that I could have believed in Father Christmas had she not been so careless.

– Halle Berry

My dad fell off the roof pretending to be a reindeer. That's how I found out.

– David, Gloucester

Alan was about to regret trying to create wonderful childhood memories for his son.

A child at school told me there was no Santa, so I beat him up for telling such dreadful lies. And then when I went to the headmistress in trouble, she confirmed the truth. I was distraught.

– Ed, Bridgnorth, Shropshire

I went to such trouble to keep the dream alive for my son. Every Christmas Eve I nibbled on carrot and spat it out to make it look like the reindeer had eaten some. I trailed sooty footprints onto the hearth, and pushed the fireguard over to look like Santa had been.

Unfortunately, one yuletide, I was in the middle of doing all this, when my 8 year-old wailed and went into what can only be described as a complete hysterical rage – he'd seen it all from the doorway!! My blood ran cold. Needless to say, Christmas wasn't great that year.

– Liz, Ealing

I knew Santa wasn't real, when I went to a car boot sale in January, and three stalls were all selling his outfits. First I wondered, 'how could there be three Santas?' Then I wondered why he was selling his outfits. Then, I realised. I could barely stand with the shock of it all!

~ Jake, Littlehampton

I was seven when I saw 'Santa' in a newsagent's shop. But my delight turned to horror when I realised he was browsing the top-shelf magazines.

~ Lydia, Portsmouth

ROUND ROBINS

The annual boast-fest was about to begin...

Hearts plummet at Christmas with the arrival of the dreaded round robin letters.

Either packed with family triumphs, sparkling children, perfect holidays and hilarious tales of talented pets, or tragedies and deaths, the 'round robin' took on a life of its own once computers allowed every Tom, Dick and Harry to become self-publishers.

Along with the general loss of judgement that happens in the festive season, 'normal' people become convinced that friends, relations and, quite frankly, almost complete strangers, will be thrilled at the news that little Amaryllis is taking her SATs four years early, and that George's new shed has changed his life. And all the better if it's gaily presented with a heavy sprinkling of seasonal imagery around the page.

No — it seems nothing is too sacred to be copied and exposed to the masses, under the guise of a cheery Christmas catch-up. Have these people no shame?!!

This letter was sent to a member of staff on a cruise ship. The American couple had spent a total of three hours in her company one week, several years ago, but stayed religiously in touch with the annual need to reveal all. Watch out for their caring, nurturing side in this lovely missive....

Happy Holidays!
This is Ike and Juanita here. Can you believe we have reached that time of year already? ... It has been an interesting year. Our daughter left her husband as he started beating up on her again. It has been difficult as we have got used to our own space. We like a drink and karaoke at night, so that had to change. Hopefully she will find a hostel soon and we can get our routine back.

(There then follows news of Ike's skin cancer, and the thrilling story of how he cut his hand open whilst opening a tin of peas)

But it's not all been bad news. We went travelling in Britain this year. Ike was attacked by a peacock at a stately home and after a long battle we got some compensation. It was enough to repair the front porch. I enjoyed having a home that looked just like other folks, but it didn't last long as Ike managed to fall asleep with a cigarette in his mouth and set fire to it. He is such a klutz!

I cannot say I'm looking forward to next year's adventures, but surely they can't be as eventful as this year's...

And then there are the little nuggets, buried within a letter that give such an insight into relationships. This poignant paragraph from a couple in London was made all the more so with the inside knowledge that they had recently taken up swinging.

...Although Charles and I have, admittedly, been through some tough patches this year, we have been seeing a counsellor. She suggested certain things for us to do together that would remind us of our commitment to each other. It has been a real learning curve – I've seen sides of him I didn't know existed...

As for elderly parents and relatives – consciences are relieved as the excuses come thick and fast in the following selection of letters…

…Caring for elderly parents is difficult. We knew the time had come to put mother into a home when she developed a penchant for hectic colour schemes. She has preferred neutral tones all her life, so we knew something was wrong…

…Toby felt sad that Granny went into a home, but we got him a rabbit, which helped…

…Father passed away in August…We went to the Caribbean in September in his memory …

42

Then on, of course, to the sparkling children. Note the ones that are particularly worthy of praise in their parents' eyes, and the unfortunates who seem to be mildly disappointing, if not downright invisible.

...Peter is a total jock – loving every minute of playing for his team. Last season he was one of the major scorers – we are so proud of him. Jim says he doesn't know where he gets it from, but I can recognise some of that twinkle in his eye, just like his father at his age (lol!) Talking of which, I think he's even got a little romance starting with one of the high school cheerleaders. And Kathy is doing well at swimming too. We've been all over the USA competing, but she says this year coming she will take some time out to be a normal teenager. I don't know how she does it! As for Sarah – well – she's fizzy and cooky as ever!!!

(The letter then gushes about the changes to their house and the new drive. Even the hamster, which has mastered the art of going round its wheel backwards, seemingly more of a high-achiever than poor old 'cooky' Sarah.)

And can't you just hear the barely-stifled pain behind this one...

...While we understand that Christmas letters are not the most appropriate time to reveal such things, it is in the spirit of love and understanding that we impart the news our son Iain is gay. Whilst we love him as much as we ever did, this has been somewhat of a shock. Peter says we should have guessed, as Ian had been collecting Waterford Crystal since he was 10...

Health features highly in many of the letters, including this lovely one from two old ladies who live together in Hull

Martha is still struggling on with her arthritis. There's little to recommend getting old. I've got type 2 diabetes now, which is a pain, but we do the best we can...The health visitor seems to be our main visitor these days, but we're thankful for her. We don't get out much due to the hill outside – after I broke my hip it was all a bit much... Anyway – we wish you all a merry Christmas and a peaceful new year.

Martha and Minnie

PS. Martha has had a perm

A slightly less cheery tone was adopted for the next letter, from a grumpy writer in London

Please excuse spelling mistakes. I have a migraine and can barely be bothered this year. But I know how people look forward to the annual catch-up.

(oh really?!)

...I gave blood for the first time this year. Imagine the excitement of discovering I'm an AB positive - the newest blood group in our species' development!!!!

But perhaps the last word should go Pat and Keith, the Birmingham Christians who covered just about every category in their eight page letter, triumphantly squeezing a biblical message into their final paragraph – Hurrah!

...And though money has been a bit tight this year, we know God will provide. And what better time than Christmas? Pat had been praying long and hard about whether to have a new carpet, when she glanced up to see a large carpet van going past the house. She took it as a sign, and we ordered one almost immediately on the internet. Proof, if it was needed that you just 'Ask and ye shall receive'!
Merry Christmas.

'TIS THE SEASON TO BE ....

*In an effort to become politically correct,
somehow the message had become tangled.*

'Tis The Season To Be...Politiically Correct

There's nothing like a good old Christian festival to bring out the PC brigade.

- In November 2005 Lambeth Council decided to rename their Christmas lights 'Winter Lights' or 'Celebrity Lights' in order not to offend other faiths.

- In Maplewood, New Jersey, school officials banned the use of traditional Christmas carols. The high school's brass ensemble was also prohibited from playing instrumental renditions of the songs – without the vocals – because as one school official put it, "if you're familiar with the tune, you know the words." No religious songs at all were performed – only non-sectarian numbers like "Frosty the Snowman" and "Walking in a Winter Wonderland."

- In one community in Massachusetts, the Mayor felt moved to send out an apology to the community saying he was wrong to identify the city's holiday party as a "Christmas" party.

- According to ACAS, holding a Christmas raffle with alcohol as prizes could offend Muslims, who should not gamble or drink.

- A detailed risk assessment was ordered for the Christmas party of the Embsay Women's Institute in Yorkshire to take into account the dangers of serving free mince pies containing suet pastry and nuts.

- In 2006 festivities in Birmingham were renamed 'Winterval'.

- Staff at the Royal Bank of Scotland were told not to put up decorations, as it could cause injury or fire. Workers wishing to hang Christmas cards on a string were also advised to book an engineer to prevent any potential claim against the company for dereliction in their duty for ensuring staff safety.

´Tis The Season To Be...Inappropriate

'Normal' behaviour goes by the wayside around this time of year. Indiscretion is the byword, with people saying and doing things they wouldn't normally do if they hadn't got a glass of wine in their hand, or a bit of mistletoe to blame it on.

Read on and cringe at these true stories.

My partner's uncle Tony (he looked like Mr Burns from 'The Simpsons') was a lonely old soul, so we had him over for Christmas one year. He had about 15% lung capacity at the best of times, but seemed to breathe easier when we gave him a whisky, so we plied him with drink and hoped for the best. We'd also invited our single friend Gael, who was around 50 years younger than uncle Tony.

We introduced them, then left them to chat while we finished preparing lunch in the kitchen. Fifteen minutes later, imagine my horror as I walked into the sitting room. Gael was sitting on a low stool on the floor, hunched over and looking terrified. Uncle Tony was breathing heavily over her, massaging her shoulders and telling her about what a great lover he had been 'in my youth'.

It was HIDEOUSLY embarrassing. We had to prise him off Gael's shoulders, and then when the drink wore off, he kept bursting into tears saying he was 'a foolish old man' and wanted to die. Very cheery!

– Rachel, London

Yorkshire people are renowned for their frankness, but my 82 year-old aunty took the biscuit when, during the family lunch, she fixed me with her beady blue eyes and asked (in a very loud voice) "You. Have you got a boyfriend yet?"

It was a very Bridget Jones-type scene, but I wasn't embarrassed and just said, "not at the moment aunty. I'm having a bit of a break in between men."

There was hardly a moment's pause when she responded, "Mmmm – don't know why you bother. These days, you could be servicing two and no-one would mind!"

There was an awful silence before everyone thankfully burst out laughing.

~ Sarah, London

Nothing was more inappropriate than my parents getting drunk and going upstairs to have noisy sex in the middle of a family party. It was so, so terrible that they haven't invited the relatives over since, and I go to my friend's every year now instead.

~ Barry, Northampton

Mum trying to be young and flirting with my friends, and adding 'innit' to the end of every sentence was fairly inappropriate.

~ Max, Peterborough

' Tis The Season To Be... injured

The chestnuts might be roasting on an open fire, but be careful they don't pop and burn you with their contents. Here's the guide to the more dangerous side of Christmas (with thanks to R.O.S.P.A.). Stats are only available up until 2002, but it's a fair guess with alcohol involved, things won't have improved.

Among the usual injuries involving exploding microwave gravy, tripping over toys, cuts from veg knives and the like. Did you know that:

- 8 Brits had serious burns in 2000 trying on a new jumper with a lit cigarette in their mouth.

- British Hospitals reported 4 broken arms in one season after 'cracker pulling' incidents.

- 31 Brits have died between 1996 and 2002 by watering their Christmas tree while the fairy lights were plugged in.

- 9 Brits have died in the 3 years 2000-2002 after believing that Christmas decorations were chocolates.

- 101 people in those 3 years had broken parts of plastic toys pulled from the soles of their feet.

- A massive 543 Brits were admitted to A&E after opening bottles of beer with their teeth.

- 5 people were injured in one yuletide season following accidents involving out-of-control Scalextric cars.

- 14 people poked their eyes badly, either whilst dressing the festive tree, or whilst catching it as it fell over.

'Tis The Season To Be...Breaking Up

The stress, the drink, the break in routine. Nothing highlights incompatibility like the festive season:

True stories ....

We were actually en-route to my parents' house, and my boyfriend was behaving like such an idiot, we ended up rowing. It got worse as we got further down the motorway, so I pulled over into a lay-by and finished with him (and left him) there and then.

~ Kally, Liverpool

I met my boyfriend's parents for the first time one Christmas. They were very lovely to my face, but when I went to the loo in the downstairs cloakroom, I heard his mum say that I was very nice, 'but you can tell where she's from the minute she opens her mouth'. I froze in horror and could hardly get through the weekend.

~ Susan, Humberside

The night my girl got so drunk she slept with three men in the office at their annual party, was when I knew it was all over for us.

~ Dave, Lincoln

My wife seemed to be out a lot during the run-up to Christmas, and I was very bored as I'd got a broken leg and was stuck in bed. Just before the big day, I spotted a loose panel underneath the base of the fitted wardrobe, so on my way to the toilet, I poked it with my plaster cast. It came away, and behind the board was a stash of money. In total, it amounted to over £10,000! And that was the beginning of how I discovered my wife had gone on the game.

~ Anon

I liked the fact my boyfriend was fun and friendly, and initially thought it was great that he was on good terms with at least a couple of his ex-girlfriends. I hate men who are bitter, so saw this as a good sign. That was until we had a Christmas party at our house and several of his exes (and mine) attended. Everyone was getting on well, drink was flowing, music was loud, loads of people dancing - just a really great atmosphere.

A bit drunk, I staggered round the house looking for Chris, feeling full of Christmas spirit and love, dying to give him a big snog. But someone had already beaten me to it. I stumbled upon him in the pantry. It was dark, but I could make out two shapes, and then I heard his voice. He was with Cally, an ex, and was telling her that he still loved her and regretted leaving her to be with me.

Because I was drunk I just reacted. I snapped the pantry light on and opened the door so everyone could see (she was sitting on the veg rack giving him a blow job), and I guess that's the moment our break up happened.

~ Effie, Wimbledon

WHEN PLANS GO ASTRAY

Albert had the wing. Now came the prayer.....

It really doesn't matter how carefully everything has been planned in advance. Sometimes, the completely unexpected can actually happen...

The day our dog Huggy Bear worked as an accomplice with the cat will remain with us forever. The cat, Shaggy, had recently perfected a manoeuvre to open the fridge by lying on her back and pawing the door open. It was hilarious, but not so funny when we got home drunk on Christmas Eve, to be greeted with a trail of skin, bone, feathers and innards through the lounge and up the stairs. It literally looked as if there had been a massacre. We both realised it was the turkey, and with horror ran upstairs (not sure what we were hoping to do at this stage), only to find the dog and cat both lying on OUR bed. They were so bloated they could only lift their heads. It became apparent they'd worked in tandem, with the cat opening the fridge, and the dog getting the turkey out. We didn't know whether to laugh or cry – and the animals didn't even have the grace to look guilty! Needless to say, Christmas dinner was just vegetables.

~ **Karen and Phil, Birmingham**

I put extra alcohol on the pudding without telling anyone... and so did my husband. When it came to lighting it, I ended up with seriously burned eyebrows.

~ Katie, London

I was in a queue for Santa, when my sister-in-law announced she was leaving my brother, for my other sister's husband. Seconds later we were called up to put my niece on Santa's lap, so we were all fake smiles and 'ho, ho, ho', while inside I was frozen with shock.

~ Jan H, Warwickshire

It was very unexpected when my dad, who was a bit worse for wear, decided to throw himself on the floor before Christmas lunch and try and breakdance. He didn't manage to breakdance, but he did break his nose as he was doing 'the caterpillar'.

~ Mike, Newquay

Having vowed I would never, ever spoil my child, I found myself queuing outside ToysRUs for a Power Ranger for my son. I was very smug and happy with my purchase, so imagine my horror when I took him to see Father Christmas the next day, and he announced he'd like Tracey Island!!! My blood ran cold. There were just two days to go. So, there I was again - phoning every store in Birmingham, and fortunately I got the last one. My son received both presents, but even then ended up playing more with a cap gun he got in his cracker.

~ Liz, Birmingham

I went to stay one Christmas with a couple who had a huge, very posh house that overlooked the entire, quaint village. They were acquaintances rather than friends, but I was grateful they'd invited me to stay as I had nothing to do. So, come Christmas day, there we were, the couple in question, and several assorted stray friends they'd decided to entertain. My first faux-pas (apparently) was not to have bought gifts for everyone – even though I didn't know them.

And the second (apparently), was to have a lie-in on Boxing Day morning. Being typically British, they'd not told me we all had to be up and gone by a certain time, so when she knocked on my door, very annoyed at 10.30 am saying 'can you get up – we've got drinks in the village at 11', I detected the Christmas spirit had well and truly left the building.

Shortly afterwards so had I - escorted to the door without so much as a cup of tea. I haven't heard from them since.

– Ruth, Birmingham

Mum deciding she'd 'had enough of Christmas, actually' on the day was not great. She refused to cook the turkey, and instead presented us with tinned steak and kidney pie that she just plonked in the middle of the table, and then went off to bed for a cry, with her words 'you all don't appreciate me' echoing round the room. I've never forgotten it.

~ Sandra, Newcastle

My mum was a Catholic convert, and took the whole shebang very seriously. Over the Christmas period she went to church three times a day and utterly exhausted herself. She also hated cooking, hated the fact that dad was drunk around 11 am and good for nothing. Consequently, the food was always disgraceful, she was always in a foul mood and it was all vile. Everyone in my family has had issues over Christmas ever since.

~ Leigh, Burnley

Travelling to visit relatives is a traditional thing, but sometimes you feel the world is telling you to stay home.

Everything was carefully organised, but bit-by-bit fell apart. My youngest daughter contracted chicken pox two weeks before, and it was touch-and-go as to whether we'd make it up North that year. I pressed on and did my baking regardless, and she seemed well enough by Dec 20th to assume it was okay. Then my son fell and broke his leg. However, it was in a cast, so we assumed it would be fine, so we continued making plans.

On the actual day, we loaded up the car, with my son on the back seat with his leg stuck out at an angle. My daughter was perched between his legs, with cushions all around them to make it comfy. Then my husband turned the ignition, but nothing happened. He spent 30 minutes tinkering (not knowing what he was doing), before we called for assistance. That took two hours to arrive, by which time we were all starving, and tucking into sandwiches (thus ruining our appetite). Then, before we got going again, we all used the bathroom for one last pee, but when my husband flushed the loo, it overflowed onto the floor. I burst into tears and gave up on the spot. We all stayed home, had more sandwiches, watched tele, and ended up really enjoying ourselves!

– Sandra, Derby

THE JOY OF GIVING

"Nothing's as mean as giving a little child something useful for Christmas." – Kin Hubbard

'...so what we do is tie these to the bottom of your shoes, and you slide up and down the kitchen floor – just like we're out skating!'

The European Crap Gifts Mountain

In December, the shops are crammed with people frantically buying things that they don't want to buy. These will be given to recipients who probably don't want or need them either.

Every year the pile of unused foot spas, car polishing kits, drug store perfumes and exercise balls grows larger. Please – don't add to the European Crap Gifts Mountain.

So if you want to avoid being known as a shite gift giver, then here are the golden rules:

- Try and like the person you are buying for.

- Don't do your 'main' shop at a car boot or trash and treasure sale.

- Don't wear it and then try to pass it off as new.

- If it comes with batteries - leave them in there!

- Don't buy a present because YOU'd love it!

- Don't buy it because the recipient will grow into it, or slim into it.

- Don't buy a giftset of something, and then split the contents between several people. That's cheap, cheap, CHEAP!!

- Don't buy 'joke' gifts when you know the other person is getting you something nice.

- Don't buy intimate, personal or embarrassing gifts that will be opened in public (ie. vaginal weights or anal bleach cream).

- Don't knit it or crochet it. Ever.

True bad gift stories...

However, if the above rules have gone unheeded, and someone has purchased you yet another foot spa or car-polishing kit, here are a few recollections to let you know you're not alone.

Back in the 70s, we got one main gift and a few smaller ones in our stockings. My main gift was late coming, and my stocking, for some reason that year, contained a tin of sardines.

~ Damian, Atlanta

My mum gave me a box of cleaning fluids, some cloths and a tin of oatcakes, saying "I know you haven't got much money, and seeing as your house is such a mess, I thought you'd appreciate this." I never figured out the oatcakes. And I never understood why she gave me the box in October.

~ Ruth, Birmingham

The worst gift is a fruitcake. There is only one fruitcake in the entire world, and people keep sending it to each other.

~ Johnny Carson

My worst present was from my sister-in-law. She gave me a floating candle fish bowl that still had the water marks on it from when she used it all year.

~ Sara, New Jersey

My dear brother got me a bottle of beer-scented bubble bath. He knows that I don't own a bath, and the Boots £1.99 price sticker could clearly be seen.

~ Steve, Worcester

I was about 13, and my grandmother actually wrapped up a box of menstrual pads and gave them to me for Xmas. I was horrified. I think it was a free sample she got in the mail, and she didn't need them anymore... I was relieved that my brother and dad were so engrossed in one of their gifts that only my mom saw it. She laughed, and nodded approvingly when I shoved them under the sofa.

~ Marcia, Lincoln

I hate stuffed toys, so why my brother bought me a LIFE-SIZED monkey, in a police uniform, complete with truncheon, I will never know. Then again, it could be explained if he'd won it at a fairground, and hadn't had to buy it at all.

~ Mary, Cannock

Aunt Jenny was a family legend. Every year, the whole family would brace ourselves for her gifts, and fake enthusiasm whilst trying to suppress the giggles and rising hysteria. However, the year she surpassed herself was when she presented my dad and his two brothers with shepherd's crooks. Unbelievable!

~ Susie, Los Angeles

Worst gift? Dental floss and tooth sticks from dad. He likes to give something practical. It was actually together with something as obscure as deer-skin slippers. They looked horrible.

~ Sarah, Wisconsin

Dropping hints about a gift is fine, but when they're picked up on years later, it's really not. I mentioned in 1995 that I might like to go to catering college. Fast-forward seven years and I was happily in a career as a secretary, having forgotten all about that whim. My aunty however, had not, and proudly presented me with a sugar thermometer (for which I had absolutely no use).

~ Helen, Nantwich

Christmas is always hilarious as my nan does her shopping at Barnardo's (and is proud of it too). She primes me, my mum and my aunty months before saying things like 'Christmas is going to be lovely for you this year. The shops have got some gorgeous things in that I've earmarked'.

And so we've made a family tradition of wearing whatever it is she gives us, and then having our photo taken in it. Our best photo was the 'green' year – mum had a green felt dress and a camoflague rucksack, my aunty had a ballgown, and I was given second-hand knickers, a green sparkly dress, a fringed cardigan and ski gloves.

~ Justine, London

Other random, hideous gifts for our poor recipients have included... Wire coat-hangers... a plastic bowl containing a note saying 'this is to be sick in'... a leopard-skin steering wheel cover for a 15 year-old... an ice shaver... a wallchart of 'Fish Of The World' (for a marine biologist)... a sack of wild bird feed for someone who had no garden... a stomach girdle for an anorexic girl.

Like we said - please don't keep adding to the Crap European Gifts Mountain.

Great Gifts

(source: Toy Retailers Association)
These are the gifts that have topped the lists of millions of kids over the past few years. Now that the Furbys have been left to turn feral in the garage, and the Alien Eggs have long-since hatched, it all seems a tad surreal. But see the names, and remember the joy of receiving them, or the stress of buying them!

Toy/Game of the Year

2006: (Toy) Dr Who Cyberman Mask (Character Group)

2005: (Toy) Tamagotchi Connexion (Bandai)

2004: (Game) Trivial Pursuit 20th Edition (Hasbro)

2003: (Toy) Beyblades (Hasbro)

2002: (Toy) Beyblades (Hasbro)

2001: (Toy) Bionicle (Lego)

2000: (Toy) Teksta (Vivid Imaginations)

Top Ten Sellers - Year 2000:

1) Scooters (generic)

2) Teksta (Vivid Imaginations)

3) Who wants to be a Millionaire? (interactive board game) (Tiger Electronics)

4) Thunderbirds Tracey Island (Vivid Imaginations)

5) Amazing Ally (Playmates)

6) Bob the Builder 12" figure (Martin Yaffe)

7) Princess Bride Barbie (Mattel)

8) Poo'chi (Tiger Electronics)

9) Pokemon Pokedex (Tiger)

10) Baby Annabel (Zapf)

Year 1999:

1) Pokemon trading cards – Wizards of the Coast (Nintendo Game Boy)

2) Furby Babies (Tiger Electronics)

3) WWF Wrestlers (Kidz Biz)

4) Who Wants To Be A Millionaire? (Upstarts)

5) Alien Eggs (Grossman)

6) Beanies (Ty)

7) Action Man Silver Speeder (Hasbro)

8) Tweenies (Hasbro)

9) Sleeping Beauty BARBIE (Mattel)

10) Baby Annabell (Zapf)

Scrooge Is Alive And Well

Heart-warming stories of those who pull out the stops to ensure every expense is spared, and good cheer is nowhere to be seen.

My gran is stinkingly rich, and this is an example of why. Amazingly, we get the same Christmas cards every year. She lets us open them, but then she collects them up ready for next year, along with all of the carefully folded, used wrapping paper from the presents.

~ Andy, Nottingham

My friend always raises the bar by handing out gifts that are beautifully wrapped and boxed. And then you open them up to find something from the local cheapo market inside. It's so disappointing.

~ Kelly, Torquay

Police in Country Durham decided the perfect time to begin clamping down on shoppers would be during the annual Christmas Eve market. Used to not having wardens on this particular patch, the locals had always been able to park where they wanted, so it came as a huge shock to find rows of freshly-issued tickets just hours before the celebrations.

Corporate Scrooge Stories:

- In 2006, the world's biggest retailer allegedly gave some employees a 20% discount coupon off one item in the store.

- One university presented employees with a food basket, containing nothing but cartons of dehydrated apple sauce.

- One bookstore held their annual party from 8am-9am, which would mean all employees coming in an hour before work officially began. Unsurprisingly, not many attended.

- One consumer electronic service engineer reports that their last annual Christmas bonus was a bag of potatoes. Apparently a relative of the boss owned a potato farm.

In 1993, Newsquest won the first 'Scrooge Award for Corporate Greed'. The Chief Executive was presented with a bag of chocolate coins, a copy of 'A Christmas Carol' and their certificate, by Jeremy Dear, General Secretary of the National Union of Journalists.

Newsquest won the award for such shameful factors as;

• Making more than $1.1b dollars worldwide (£70m in the UK), but paying many of its journalists as little as £12,000 per annum.

• Pressurising many journalists to sign opt-outs of health and safety legislation

• Giving below-inflation pay awards, whilst many executives took rises of up to 43%!!!

• Needless to say, corporate gifts to their employees weren't even in evidence.

TRIVIA

Facts and Figures

- In the UK, one billion cards end up in bins across the country. It takes one tree to make approximately 3,000 cards, so that's 333,333 trees felled.

- 7 million children leave mince pies and a drink for Santa on Christmas Eve.

- Nearly 3,000 tonnes of aluminium foil will be used to wrap turkeys.

- In the USA the National Retail Federation estimates that up to 6 percent of gifts are returned the week following Christmas.

- 8,000 Christmas trees will be thrown away, generating 12,000 tonnes of rubbish.

- 125,000 tonnes of plastic packaging will be binned – the equivalent in weight to 50,000 polar bears!

- In Bergen, Norway, inhabitants take part in building the world's biggest gingerbread city. Every school, kindergarten or individual that wants to can take part, and their offerings are then taken to the local mall. Here the constructions, schools, buildings, houses, boats, people are put on display to form the world's biggest gingerbread city.

- Mince pies date back to medieval times and possibly long before. They are descended from a huge pie baked on Christmas Eve, containing chopped beef, suet, nuts, spices and fruit of which whole dried plums were an important constituent. The pie was originally baked open, but as time wore on a crust was added, on top of which a pastry effigy of the infant Jesus was laid to represent him lying in his cradle.

- An extra 750 million glass bottles and jars will be used over the Christmas period.

- The UK spends £20bn on Christmas with £1.6bn going on food and drink.

- To obtain a UK number one song, you'd normally need to sell only around 20,000 units. At Christmas, this rises to around 250,000.

- Christmas 2000 saw the UK consuming 10 million turkeys, 25 million Christmas puddings, 250 million pints of beer and 35 million bottles of wine.

- Children have to wait until January 6th for their gifts in Italy, when they are, according to tradition, delivered by a kind, ugly witch called Befana.

- Approximately 380,000 people will be homeless each Christmas in the UK.

WHY DO WE DO IT?

Kitsch is in at Christmas... Oh no it isn't! Oh yes it is!!

*Someone had put 'Save Your Love' by Renee and Renato
on the jukebox again.*

The festive season and the novelty record...what is it about the British and their need to bung rubbish on their sound systems at yuletide? With a much larger music-buying demographic than normal, anything has a chance of making number one - especially if your mad granny has a say in it!

But it's not just grannies... it's neighbours having parties, drunk uncles with no idea of what to buy you, the Secret Santa £10 shopping limit people from work - on it goes.

Somehow, because it's Christmas, guests at gatherings worldwide are subjected to this dross. Past offenders of the highest order include:

1949
All I Want For Christmas Is My Two Front Teeth

~ Spike Jones and The City Slickers

Amazingly, this song was by music teacher Don Gardner in 30 minutes, when he noticed that most of his class had at least one front tooth missing. Spike Jones recorded it and took it to the top of the charts in early 1949, but it went on to be covered many times by artists including Nat King Cole, The Andrews Sisters and even the cast of Sesame Street. There's even a rap parody by Cledus T Judd on his 2002 album entitled 'All I Want For Christmas Is Two Gold Front Teef'. Innit.

1970
Two Little Boys

~ Rolf Harris

Unbelievably, this desperate morality tale of Jack and Joe, two boys growing up together, kept Elvis and his Suspicious Minds off the number one slot. . One of the boys breaks his wooden horse, so the other offers to share his. The favour is then returned years later, during the civil war, when Joe helps an injured Jack onto his horse ('Do you think I would leave you crying, when there's room on my horse for two?'), and off to safety. Once recovered, they both realise they are in love, and trailblaze for homosexual rights throughout the USA.

Actually, I'm making that last bit up as it's more interesting.

1971
Ernie

~ Benny Hill

The 'musical' equivalent of a saucy British seaside postcard, this
innuendo-laden song tells the story of Ernie the milkman and his
nemesis, the breadman Two-Ton Ted from Teddington. This
hideous, hideous story (have I emphasised that enough?)
describes their rivalry for the heart of a widow called Sue, and
culminates in a street battle, using only weapons from their
respective vans. Like an early Kanye West or 50 cent, these boys
fight to the end, but Ernie is felled by a rock-cake, swiftly
followed by a pork pie to the eye. But Ernie gets even when he
comes back to haunt them on their wedding night – thus
fulfilling his ultimate fantasy giving Sue the willies.

There's No-one Quite Like Grandma

~ St Winifred's School Choir

This choir, composed of sugary little girls in pink uniform and a toothless ginger one at the front, stormed the charts. Fantastically marketed to appeal to kids and grannies alike, it sold in bucketloads, as it was the ideally priced gift to bung granny's way. Extolling the virtues of granny, the subversive message was hidden in verse two:

> There's no-one quite like Grandma
> She always has a smile
> She never hurries us along
> Just stays a little while

'Just stays a little while'? How ungrateful can you get? All that love and guidance they were twittering about earlier in earlier verses, and they can't be bothered to spend more than an hour with her. Poor gran - cast aside like a lavender and pee-scented doll that's fallen out of favour. Let's hope those wicked girls of St Winifred's, who will

all be in their 30s now, have learned some remorse!

~ Bob The Builder (& Friends)

Can he fix it? Yes he can! And he did – to reach number one, beating Westlife to the coveted spot, and knocking off Eminem with 'Stan'. Wouldn't it have been so much more exciting to have celebrated Christmas to a backdrop about an obsessive, girlfriend-murdering fan? Instead, we got Bob and his delightfully-named mates Scoop, Muck and Dizzy and Roley too, getting busy fixing things as new. Slightly puzzling was the declaration that

> Bob and the gang make a really good sound
> Working all day till the sun goes down

Now call me naive, but I've yet to meet a builder who makes a 'really good sound'. Could it have been something of a more adult nature – maybe the visit to the site by Wendy, Bob's friend (but probably the hod-carrier's 'ho'), earlier on in the song?

Other Offenders Include:

I Farted on Santa's Lap (Now Christmas is Gonna Stink for Me)

~ **The Little Stinker**

Jingle Bells

~ **Singing Dogs**

Grandma Got Run Over By A Reindeer

~ **Elmo and Patsy**

I Saw Daddy Kissing Santa Claus

~ **Kip Addota**

And The Unforgettable:

Twenty Tiny Fingers

~ The Stargazers

A nauseating song about the birth of twins

A Wombling Merry Christmas

~ The Wombles

Reaching number two, these hirstute creatures sang of the joys of 'wombling in the snow', which doesn't make the slightest bit of sense. Do Wombles womble? Do we care? Did we ever...

Mr Blobby

~ **Mr Blobby**

I feel too ill to comment!

Say 'Eh-Oh'

~ **The Teletubbies**

Save Your Love

~ Renee and Renato

Possessive UK-based Italian tenor and English girl warble disturbingly at each other, completely disregarding cultural barriers in this missive of hope.

Long Haired Lover From Liverpool

~ Jimmy Osmond

Slightly disturbing that a nine year-old would be singing about such things. But its incongruity was lost on the public who liked the idea of a pre-pubescent child promising to 'do anything you say'.

Panto Time

With a rich and varied history, panto has been delighting children (and secretly adults) for years. With its roots in music hall, it then moved on to theatre, where it became more respectable, despite men dressing as women and seeming to enjoy it a tad too much. Here are a few true stories to bring it even more alive.

According to comic Jimmy Tarbuck, there's a famous story that happened at the Oxford Apollo in 1985. Apparently Cilla Black left a gap in her defences when she appealed to the audience with the question 'Boys and girls. How am I going to kill this terrible villain?'
To which one kid shouted out, 'Just sing to him'.

It's traditional on the last night of panto, for the cast to play jokes on each other, so the cast and the audience are always primed to expect the unexpected. But the principal boy went a tad too far in one performance, when she strutted on stage to be greeted by a fellow actor asking quizzically

'Aha! Puss in boots?'

To which she replied - 'No. They don't reach that high'

There was an audible gasp from the adults, followed by hoots of laughter.

A similarly naughty happening occured at The Weston Playhouse in 1990, when Man Friday, a very fit black man by the name of Oscar, lost his leopardshin loin cloth, only to discover that his accompanying g-string wasn't doing the job it was made for. Everyone saw more than they'd bargained for, but the pro that he was, Oscar carried on doing his solo breakdance, whilst adjusting himself in time to the beat.

During the same panto (which had a particularly colourful cast that year), there was a very public sacking, when it became apparent that the the 'comic' who played the character of Billy Crusoe – wasn't actually funny.

Billy was the last person to notice (so often the way), but when he did, he began to put coping mechanisms into place, which happened about halfway through the season. By this time, when he started going badly, he simply resorted to fainting on the spot. The first time it happened everyone laughed, then it fell silent as everyone realised it wasn't in the script, and the curtains closed on a stunned audience, whilst everyone backstage frantically decided what to do.

The second time, the cast were prepared. When Billy fell to the floor, Captain Hook (who was also the director, came on (still in character), hoiked Billy's stray arm from the edge of the stage with his cane and announced loudly,

'He's not funny, he's out of time
His contract's up, and so's this rhyme'

Billy continued feigning unconsciousness, which was probably his best bit of acting throughout the whole season.

However, often it's the props that let you down, as one well-known actor found during panto in Liverpool. Not renowned for his speed of wit, nobody could ever have guessed that he'd win the day. Charged with just four lines in one scene, he had to utter a curse, and then, if everything went according to plan, his enemy would disappear down a trap door.

On the fated night, he began his rhyme:

'I have got a tale to tell.
Puss will soon be down the well.
And as for our young Sonny Jim
You have seen the last of him!"

Unfortunately, the flashpaper did not fire (the electrician had buggered off), and the trapdoor only half opened. The villain tried again, with the same result.

Then, starting everyone, including himself, he turned to the audience and uttered the immortal lines;

'Goodness gracious what a caper
Someone's pissed on the magic paper!'

He marched off to huge applause. Truly the spirit of great panto!

Jimmy Tarbuck On Showbiz

The A-Z Of A Crap Christmas

A – Arguments

Practically obligatory. Everything from whose house you're going to spend Christmas at, to how much to spend on the children; when to put the tree up; what party to go to; why were you looking in that way at that person during such and such a party; how come so much is on the credit card and can't you turn the noise down I'm trying to sleep. Marvellous for those suffering from low-blood pressure.

B – Boredom

Usually sets in mid-afternoon on Christmas day. The food is eaten, bellies are bloated, small-talk is made and the same films are on TV again. Difficult to hide, tell-tale signs include yawning, long sighs and glazed expressions. Antidotes include leaping up off the sofa to make tea, disappearing upstairs for 'a quick nap', suggesting a board game or, preferably, going home.

C – Coach Trips

Stupid activity that takes you to Christmas markets all over the continent. Group singing is often forced upon the participants en-route. On arrival, passengers are dispersed and given several hours to buy pointless carved wooden toys, candy sticks and naff bits of jewellery, whilst imbibing far too much mulled wine before being herded back home. The whole event is punctuated by gleeful narrative from over-cheerful guides hoping for a large tip. Book early to avoid disappointment!

D - Drink

And we're not talking the soft stuff. Drink brings out the best and worst in people, but it's very necessary to get through the season. Warning signs you've had too much include telling everyone you 'bloody love' them, involuntary urination, thinking a fight would be 'quite nice', and offering 'honest' advice to people who haven't requested it.

E - Egg Nog

In other countries it would be against your human rights to have to drink this stuff.

F - Families

American Carol Nelson once said 'Christmas is a time when you get homesick – even when you're home'. Never has a truer word been spoken. At no other time of the year would we choose to be with a bunch of people we know so well, but don't know at all. With the rise of the nuclear family, and second and third families – whole swathes of people are thrown together with about as much in common as the guests on Jerry Springer's show.

G – Greed

We eat like starving dogs at a bin bag, and then spend the rest of the afternoon distended with wind, trying to silently expel it, whilst swearing we'll never do it again. Then an hour later, someone breaks open the chocs, passes round a bowl of nuts, and we're off again.

We know it's supposed to be a representation of the three kings, but really? Who do you know who ever looked good in one? Generally bald people take on the characteristics of The Thunderbirds, while people with long hair tend to look like Afghan hounds. Whichever way, it's a bad look.

I – Ice Skating

A nice family bonding activity that can often result in severed fingers and bruised buttocks. Thanks to global warming, ice has been thinner than ever on many ponds and rivers, resulting in more folks falling down cracks and disappearing, than ever before.

J – Jokes

Aaargh to all that crap, forced seasonal jollity. And as for jokes in crackers... who gives a toss why the man got the sack from the orange juice factory (because he couldn't concentrate)? Very few people are naturally funny, and if they think a slip of paper in a cracker is going to make them more popular – then think again!

Related by blood or marriage, this is a tricky one. Slightly further down the ladder than those with titles of close family/relative, you might not see this branch from one year to the next, but seasonal obligations set in, and suddenly you're faced with the dilemma. To buy or not to buy? To invite or not to invite? And what the feck to talk about if you do meet up? Indeed, you know so little about these people, you may as well blindfold yourself, totter out into the street and invite home the first person you bump into. Recommended tactics to avoid interaction include faking your own death or catching something highly contagious. If you absolutely have to issue an invite, employ reverse-psychology and make sure it contains a family photo of you all looking pasty and ill and include a self-indulgent round-robin and a disgustingly-themed menu ('I thought we'd have an original Victorian Christmas this year. What fun!'). Hopefully they'll be the ones making the excuses, leaving you to enjoy your seasonal highlights with your 'real' family.

L – Lapland

The latest 'in' destination for holidays and pre-Christmas treats for kids. Meet Santa, see his Grotto, buy his very expensive souvenirs. Beware, too, of the rise of competitive seasonal holidaying

M – Meltis Newberry Fruits

Little sugary sacks of evil that personified Christmas for years. Looking temptingly like an American Hardgum, they shocked you with their liquid centres which were so sweet they could send one into an instant diabetic coma. Discontinued in the 1990s, they have now made their way back onto shelves again.

The stress of making the outfits, the heartbreak of seeing little Nigella squeezed into the story playing a blade of grass the donkey eats en-route to Bethlehem. The boredom of the other kids' performances, the horror of seeing one of the angels on the back row grabbing at his crotch because he needs a wee. Not recommended for your average parent to have to go through more than once.

O – Office Parties

A real test of the team player. Guaranteed to weed out office sneaks, brown-nosers and those who can't hold their drink. Danger spots include stationery cupboards, photocopiers and any office that is lockable. Total purgatory for those who don't enjoy their work or like their colleagues. And then there's the drudgery of having to find a new job afterwards...

P – Panto

What a mixed-up nation we are! Find your husband in a pair of your knickers and it's a tragedy and you divorce him. See a man on stage in full drag and red lipstick, you pay £25 for the privilege and say it was a great show! Is this any example to the kids?!

Q – Queues

On a night out? Join the queue outside the club/theatre/restaurant. Looking for those last-minute gifts – join the queue at the tills. Need a cab home – join the queue at the taxi rank. Everywhere are crowds and throngs and queues. Good enough reason to stay at home with your Meltis Newberry Fruits and watch the world go by.

R – Restaurant Prices

What a treat – the whole family are having Christmas day out. But what's this? Suddenly, the menu has quadrupled in price. Full traditional Christmas dinner (which was on the carvery last week as 'Roast Turkey Sunday lunch' at £12.50), is now an entirely reasonable £38.50. And a bottle of house wine to wash it all down? That'll be £27.00 please.

S – Secret Santa

Oh joy! You've got a £10 limit and you've drawn Mrs Mulligatawney from Customer Services. You've only met her once, and that was when you had to take her on one side and have a word about her BO. That rules out the option of any kind of toiletry (which is about all you can buy these days for £10). At 17 stone, she's probably not the g-string type either, so it's looking grim. Oh what to buy? And why do the management put us through this charade every year? Aaargh...!

T – Twelve Days Of Christmas

Why doesn't someone start a campaign to make it just one or two days at the most?

U – Unexpected Visitors

Sometimes welcome, sometimes not, but whatever the situation, the thought that a group of people may land on you at any time puts huge pressure on you to have a fully-stocked fridge and larder at all times. You may spend hundreds of pounds in anticipation and never receive a single impromptu guest, but it's a risk and expense you have to take.

Look at her dress / Who does she think she's looking at? / Oh my God – don't look now but who is that woman on Heathcliffe's lap? / Damn – it's aunty bloody Rita on the doorstep / Well I don't normally like to say anything but... / And you'd think he knew me better than to buy me a folding table tennis table wouldn't you?

Yes – it's the season of goodwill to all men again...

W – Wise Men

Usually hard to find three in one place, especially when drink is involved.

X – Xmas Specials

Television repeats that are shown year after year after year. Usually billed as 'old favourites', hasn't anyone realised this actually means they are no longer 'current' favourites?

Y – Yuletide Logs

Sickly roulard-type dessert that nobody likes, but everyone feels they should have on their table to make it more festive.

Z – Zealots (Religious or otherwise)

Constantly on hand to remind us of the true meaning of Christmas, the religious zealot has that uncanny knack of making us all feel guilty about being so old-baggish about the whole thing. They must be avoided at all costs!

The Christmas Resistance Movement

A group of anti-Xmas subversives exist out on the weird, wonderful world of the web.

Join them at www.xmasresistance.org. But here's a taster of their website and some of the comments from their message board.

Xmas resistance says:

Christmas, to early Christians was about as significant a religious holiday as St. Filbert's Day. Read "The Trouble With Christmas" by Tom Flynn, an unusually well-researched history of the holiday. We're all for Christians celebrating it the "traditional" way – which was to virtually ignore it.

"It's not really Christmas that should be boycotted, but the marketing artefacts of 'The Season' and 'The Holidays.' You must have noticed that the word 'Christmas' has become anathema to the merchandisers. It is rarely mentioned explicitly in advertising. Their desire to exploit 'The Holidays' and 'The Season' as a reason for vulgar consumption has become much more universal."

– St. Stephen

Xmas resistance says:

A strange ritual takes place during the Xmas season:
People pull out the previous year's list of Xmas card
recipients, and decide whether they still care enough
to send another card to everyone. Some people get
crossed off the list, or demoted to digital greeting
cards. This is supposedly done to celebrate a season
of love.

"What about cards? What's wrong with just sending
cards? Some of them are even made from recycled
paper. Also, I can send cards on the web for free!"

- Henny

Xmas resistance says:

It's amazing how some people won't bother keeping in touch with others, yet still make an effort to buy gifts for them. How can the gift itself be anything but prepackaged landfill? The money would be better spent on phone calls during those other 364 days, or even (*gasp!*) actually coming to visit!

"Last year I got a phone call from a relative, telling me off for not wanting to come down and be with the family. Odd. There are 364 other days that the phone doesn't ring. I gave up on Christmas a long time ago and two years ago cut my ties with this consumptive holiday of greed and mental mal-alignment."

– Doc

Xmas resistance says:

We know a few sheep, and they've informed us that December 25th is not a time when shepherds watch their flocks by night. So "Christ" never WAS in "Christmas," which may be why the name's been replaced by an "X". We are working hard to put the "Satan" back into "Satanta," though.

"I figure the most subversive thing one can do on Xmas is to sleep through it."

– Justin

"The Xmas rituals are developed from the original Siberian shaman's sacred mushroom rituals (Amanita muscaria), the familiar large red mushoom cap with white dots. From the reindeer to the stringing over the hearth and the coniferous tree with magical gifts appearing overnight under the branches (the Amanita muscaria could be said to be the fruit of the coniferous tree)... actually the list goes on much longer."

– Odin

Xmas resistance says:

We thought Santa's robes were red because of a deal he cut with a certain cola manufacturer, but your information is intriguing, to say the least. Satanta, on the other hand, is red hot for entirely different reasons.

Great Websites and Societies

(information current and correct at time of going to press)

www.welovechristmaslights.com
The site of a couple called Jeff and Lynda Womack in Schertz, Texas. Their entire existence seems to be to use up the state's supply of electricity.

www2.b3ta.com/merrychristmas
Tramp O Claus
Highly offensive and hilarious animation of tramp/father Xmas on park bench, spewing his vitriol at the world

http://www.wiiarcade.com/play/tangerine-panic-xmas/
Tangerine Panic Xmas
Online game where you have to help Santa avoid the falling tangerines

www.uglychristmaslights.com
Does what it says on the tin

www.pulpshop.co.uk
A site where you can purchase a lovely selection of 'I hate Christmas' cards

www.youtube.com
A Very Cynical Christmas

SCROOGE
Society to Curtail Ridiculous Outrageous and Ostentatious Gift Exchanges

ACKNOWLEDGMENTS

With grateful thanks to the following publications, organisations and websites, which provided small amounts of content or large amounts of inspiration during the course of research:

Kindly Leave The Stage (The Story of Variety 1919 – 1960) by Roger Wilmut.
Published by Methuen, London.

Tarbuck on Showbiz – by Jimmy Tarbuck.
Published by Willow Books, London

comedy-zone.net

www.emailsanta.com

www.funnystuff.co.uk

www.bbc.co.uk

www.southlondon.co.uk

www.aclj.org/news

www.yorkshirepost.co.uk

www.thisislondon.co.uk

www.the idler.co.uk

www.dmoz.org

www.recyclingconsortium.org.uk

www.britishturkey.co.uk

The Internet movie database (www.imdb.com)

www.xmasresistance.org

The National Union of Journalists, www.nuj.org.uk

www.christmassantaclaus.com

www.onlineweb.com